You Are Specific

(Don't Lose Yourself)

KWABENA EDDIE MANKATA

ISBN: 9988-2-2813-2

ISBN-13: 978-9988-2-2813-2

DEDICATION

To my big brother Frederick Nyinaku and wife Elsie
Nyinaku and their three beautiful kids. Thank you for the
love and support..

CONTENTS

The sovereign LORD has given me the capacity to be his spokesman, so that I know how to help the weary. He wakes me up every morning; he makes me alert so I can listen attentively as disciples do.

-Isaiah 50:4(NET)

ACKNOWLEDGMENTS

God – My creator and director. How marvellous are your works. I thank you for my hands, feet, eyes, nose; I thank you for how incredibly specific I am.

Adjoa Anobea, Akosua Agyeibea, Yaw Obiri, Ewurafua Okyerebea & Sarah Larbi – I see a beautiful difference in us.

Asantes, Ntis, Aforlas, Barnies & Boiquayes - You are enough proof family isn't always blood.

Akworkor Okutu – God created you with me in mind. You inspire me in ways no one else does. Thank you.

Akosua Aduboahene, Clifford Appiah-Kubi, Desmond Agyemang, Joseph O. Boadi, Stanley Amon, Priscilla Mensah and Tracy Pappoe – Beautiful how we began. I see a great end. Keep your eyes fixed on the Jesus.

Benedict Sarpong, Felix Okley, Emmanuel Debrah, Sween H. Ofori and Ernest Marfo – My able supports who make me look like a superman. God has set divine paths for you. Stay close to Him.

Selorm David Aforla - If David had Jonathan. I have you!

Dede Sackey & Anne Tawiah - You spot the inconspicuous errors I missed. God has every tiny area of your lives covered. Keep rising.

Nehemiah K. Paul and Gabriel Agbagba - Long hours of editing, debating and sharing jokes. I can't say thanks enough. Stay true guys.

Pentecost International Worship Centre, Sakumono Family – Each of you, I am grateful to fellowship with every time. Thanks to the leadership for the support and encouragement. A Living Church indeed!

Class of 2000 Seven Great Academy, Life Theatre and Royal Vine Theatre Ministries – How time flies whenever we meet. Let's continue to work God's agenda.

Apostle Emmanuel Offei Ankra–Badu, Pastor Jonathan Kofie and Pastor Christian Tsekpoe (Church Of Pentecost), Rev Jonathan Ekuban (Spring of Life Chapel) Pastor Prince Nyarko (ICGC, Kharis Temple) and Pastor Isaac Mensah (Fountain Gate, Glory Pastures) - God bless you for your diverse supports and guidance.

The Mankata Studios Family - What a blend of individual distinctiveness! We are doing this till Jesus comes. Love you all.

Naserian Jeanne and Abigail Acheampong – Thanks for the poems. I pray your words continually touch millions. Keep writing.

Joseph Bart-Plange – Beautiful cover and layout design. You are specific. The world is for your taking.

And you, dearest reader – Remain stubborn to your uniqueness in God.

INTRODUCTION

Beauty is the sight of the sun setting. It is the nightly view of the stars when lying in the grass. It is the melodious tunes of birds at the break of dawn. The whisper of insects. The roar of thunder. The race of lightning. The whistle of wind. The dancing of leaves. The rise of tides. Beauty is the intentional specifics of nature which render words inadequate to describe its creator; God.

Now pause to consider the greatest work of God. What do you think? Don't answer. To be God's best is simply inexplicable. Argument settled. You and I are specific. Not an afterthought. Not a rush through. Not an experiment. Not an inch shorter or taller at a certain age. Not too dark or too white. Everything about us was carefully thought through from the end to the beginning. Yeah, from the end to the beginning.

Yet the world is trying to make us think otherwise. The devil keeps whispering inadequacy and contempt. He keeps preying on our emotions and desires. Sadly, he appears to be succeeding. We have and are constantly throwing ourselves into roles we think best suits us. We are doing anything to feel beautiful, satisfied and accepted. Truthfully, we don't fit. We don't, no matter how hard we try or lie to ourselves.

And the results are resentments, envy, unhealthy competitions and devious acts taking front seat in homes, institutions and organizations even within Christian circles. We don't realise how specific we are individually. We are forcing ourselves to stand out when we are already outstanding in Christ.

You don't think God knew you and about fifty people within your community could sing, write, speak, act, pastor a church, play the piano, be a lawyer, designer and run a business etc. but created you? He did. Yet He made you specific. Same with your assignment here. With each individual comes a certain uniqueness tailored for a specific assignment.

You are a part of a whole. You are here to reflect the glory of God. You do that by completing the work given to you by God. And eventually repeat the words of Jesus, "I have brought you glory on earth by completing the work you gave me to do."[1]

You are specific. Each child of God has a unique role. God doesn't double cast. You are about to find out how intentional God is about you and then celebrate our differences. All for a reason to reflect God's glory. You are specific. Let's begin. Be Inspired!

1 DO YOU REMEMBER?

It was a Tuesday evening. The Seventeenth of June in the year Two Thousand and Fourteen. I was at Sakumono Estate Junction (Tema, Ghana) Bus Terminal with several public transport bus drivers. We were watching the El Tri of Mexico frustrate the Selecaó of Brazil in the third Group A Match at the World Cup held in Brazil. First half was almost over with no goals from either side. The statistics placed the Brazilians ahead in terms of possessions and shots at goal. Yet Memo Ochoa; the Mexican goalkeeper had become a goliath. The Brazilians hadn't found their David yet.

The commentary was eclipsed by lots of arguments. Arguments by the drivers. Arguments among groups of three and four all over. There were several motions on board argued for and against. In one group, was the fluidity of the Brazilian team. Another, the swiftness of the Mexican team. Some, the bias of Fifa. The rest talked about the history of the World Cup.

Shout, and you increase your chances of winning the argument. And if you won, your opponent would be listening attentively until you make an absurd or false statement then another one begins. It was amusing because as a football fan, I noticed deceptions. I noticed incomparable comparisons argued with vigour, confidence and passion. They were too many to correct so I stood aside. I concentrated on the moving pictures with a different sound. It was uncomfortable but manageable.

Soon the first half was over. They didn't bother listening to the constructive criticisms and suggestions by the analysts in the studio. They kept on arguing till the second half began.

Then all the arguments ceased. All eyes were glued to the television set. Something unimaginable was on the screen. All the Mexican players came back dressed as goalkeepers. They stood in front of their goal post. All eleven in the goal post!

Perhaps the players thought, "Why not further frustrate these Brazilians?" Or even their fans suggested the idea. It mattered not who did. After the recess, they were on the pitch as goalkeepers. The Brazilians rushed to the referee. Their looks and gestures were bold enough to register their displeasure even if the referee was deaf. Their fans started coming onto the pitch. The police couldn't control them. The match had to end immediately. It was all over the major and minor news networks. All over social media. It was unimaginable.

Do you remember? No? Really? Not even a little? Good! It didn't happen. Second half was played and the match ended goalless.

All eleven players as goalkeepers? No! Nothing like that has ever happened in soccer. Not even for the soccer matches played late Monday afternoons at the Sakumono School Complex Park closer to my home.

Who will ever think of that? No one! Such act will mar the beauty of the game. It will punch holes in the sanity of a well-accepted sport.

Pause for moment! Think of the earth as a playing field. You, a player in a position assigned by God. Owing to the way He created you, you are given left back position. You are created specifically for that role. Your success in that position will follow surely like goodness and mercy in Psalm twenty three. That's how God designed it.

Then one day you decided based on suggestions from friends, fans and family to be a goalkeeper. Guess how many balls you will collect from your net at the end of your first match? Try. The last person to be angry at you will be you.

We mar the beauty of God's divine plan for us when we decide to be someone else. When we decide to do something other than what's meant for us. When we don't see our values. When we lower our worth by worldly reasoning. When we allow the world to dictate to us.

This world which makes us feel like square pegs in round holes when we are actually round pegs in round holes. This world which makes us feel like cripples though we have all limbs intact. This world which makes us feel worthless when we are everything to God.

Did God make a mistake with you? Were you a pilot project? Oh Shoot! Did God forget to add a sweet voice? Or was He tired when it got to your turn? The answer to all these questions is NO. Read the words of King David below

"For you created my inmost being; you knit me together in my mother's womb. I praise you because I am fearfully and wonderfully made; your works are wonderful. I know that full well. My frame was not hidden from you when I was made in the secret place. When I was woven together in the depths of the earth, your eyes saw my unformed body." **Psalm 139: 13-15**

Here is the fact. God took His time with you. He made you in His own image.[1] God did what He knows how to do best with you. You are the most magnificent, the most extraordinary, the most wonderful and the most splendid being God has ever created. He made one kind of you. There is no mold box for another to be created same as you. There can't be a duplicate. That will be an indictment

5

on the creativity of God who even has innumerable species of birds. You are undoubtedly special.

You are specific. You aren't an accident. You aren't a mistake. You aren't a decision of an uncontrolled emotional moment. You were planned. God had you in mind before He painted the sky blue. He thought of your nose before He decided leaves should be green. He had your beauty in mind before He gave scales to fishes. God gave David skills to play the harp before He gave tunes to the mocking bird. Same as you, God was and is still intentional about you.

You are specific. Your shoe size and height from birth to death is known. Your numbered hairs and those that fall by the day are recorded. The tooth you lost. The nails you cut. The tears you shed. Everything is known by God.

You are more than what some study conducted about Monday born or the rest of the six days born say you are. There is much more in you than what they say about August borns or any of the other eleven months. Don't buy the description you are dumb because you are black. You are quick tempered because you are short. Your value is because of a certain star. Your identity is born out of the universe. They are all lies. You are specific. Hand crafted by God.

The school you attended. Your place of birth. Where you work. Your job position. These may give you bragging rights for fun. They don't define you. Don't make them.

Recently on the internet are sites that attempt to define who we are. When you visit these sites and fill out a questionnaire, you are told what career you were meant for, who has a crush on you, how you would look in about fifty years' time, what your name and profile pictures says about your personality etc. People visit to take their identity and value from such conclusions. You see man's attempt to define the divinely created? Funny. Don't fall for it. Your definition is given by God.

You are specific. Born to your family, nation and

continent by a careful divine selection. Given a skin complexion for reasons that far transcends beauty and glamour. Assigned special gifts and talents for deeper reasons than fame and fortune. Given a gender that goes beyond inner satisfaction and outward appreciation.

St Augustine said, "Men go abroad to wonder at the height of mountains, the huge waves of the sea, the long course of rivers, the vast compass of the ocean, the circular motion of the stars but they pass by themselves without wondering."[2] Be awed by the unique piece of creation you are.

People will describe you by many standards. Sometimes by your appearance; complexion, height, weight etc. Sometimes by your profession; author, teacher, banker and many more. Sometimes by your personality; kind, gentle, quick tempered, emotional etc. Sometimes one moment of weakness becomes your name tag. The man who cheated on his wife. The ex-convict down the road. The disgraced church leader. The failed politician. Yet none of these definitions divinely fits you.

One time, Eliab had quite a description of his brother David. He only saw pride and naughtiness of heart. Even their father Jesse, forgot about David when Samuel attended his household to anoint a King. Yet that specifics of God about David didn't change.[3] He was created a song writer, poet, soldier and King. He became all.

Sometimes you use your inabilities, weaknesses and challenges to describe yourself. You don't have to voice it out. You know you hold a mental ill-description of yourself. I have done it before. Yet not a single one of these descriptions is true. You aren't what you think you are. You are what God says you are.

Don't let anyone make you feel less of God's description of you. Don't feel sorry for being what God created you to be. Don't cower under inadequacy or low self-esteem. Anytime you feel short of anything, here is what to do. Build a ladder out of that feeling and climb to tap into God's grace. God asks that we therefore come boldly to the throne of grace, that we may obtain mercy and find grace in time of need.[4] You are a new creation in Christ. Your kind is made for heaven. You are specific.

Comparisons will make you feel less of everything. Less attractive! Less intelligent! Less gifted! Comparison is a mirror which reflects inadequacy no matter what you put in front of it. Comparison will outline your fears. It will bolden your shortcomings. It will leave you sad. It will lead you to question God. It will stagnate you. I know so. I have suffered it. If you are there, may I submit to you your fears don't define you. Your shortcomings don't mar your beauty. Your weaknesses don't even surprise God. He made you. Don't compare yourself to anyone. You are specific.

God has made provisions for the weaknesses. Provisions for the low moments in life. For when sadness and depression set in. For when we are in need. The provision is the Holy Spirit.

His responsibility is to comfort. Elaborating on His responsibility means to counsel, help, advocate, intercede, strengthen and standby you to stay true to your God given specification no matter what.[5] In the same way, the Spirit helps us in our weaknesses. We don't know what we ought to pray for, but the Spirit Himself intercedes for us with groans that words cannot express. And he who searches our hearts knows the mind of the Spirit, because the Spirit intercedes for the saints in accordance with God's will.[6] Isn't God good?

Paul, writing to the Corinthians mentioned a weakness for which he sought the Lord thrice to remove. God's response to him is same for us today, "My grace is sufficient for you, for my strength is made perfect in weakness."[7]

And how can you possibly think God doesn't love you? How can you fall for such deception? Wait, who hates his most cherished creation? Think about it. Why will God sacrifice His only son to restore a relationship we rather broke? Find me a reason that best explains this move than love. If death can't break His love, you think a slip will? You think a bad call will? You think a wrong judgment will? God is madly in love with you. He wants you to remain in Him. Come back to Him when you fall. His hands are opened to you. You know why? You are specific.

So get up. Dust yourself off any form of pity. You are specific blessed with every spiritual blessing in heavenly places. No one gets anywhere magnifying their weaknesses. Don't let your weakness dictate your pace. Talk to the Holy Spirit.

Read your Bible often. It is the manual for keeping your freshness in the Lord. It means the opinions of others don't count. Your feelings don't count. Only what God says counts. Let's scan a few scriptures to confirm your worth.

"You, dear children are from God and have overcome them, because the one who is in you is greater than the one who is in the world." **1 John 4:4**

"Now if we are children. Then we are heirs- heirs of God and co-heirs with Christ, if needed we share in his sufferings in order that we may also share in his glory." **Romans 8:17**

"But you are a chosen people, a royal priesthood, a holy nation, God's special possession, that you may declare the praises of Him who called you out of darkness into his wonderful light." **1 Peter 2:9**

"But our citizenship is in heaven. And we eagerly await a Savior from there, the Lord Jesus Christ." **Philippians 3:20**

You were made to stand out. No one can talk like you.

No one can write like you. No one can sing like you. No one can act like you. You can be imitated but no one can get it exact as you. God knows everything about you. You are too precious to be altered in anyway. You are whole. Be energized by the Holy Spirit. Lift your head high. That's it! Now run your race on the wheels of grace! You are specific. Be Inspired!

2 SPECIFIC FOR A PURPOSE

Being fully aware you are specific begs the reason God created you. For God who is the master creator, meticulous planner and impeccable timer; it is highly inconceivable He will somehow throw us on earth to add up to the statistics, wander about and decide for ourselves whatever we want. Even parents plan their children's lives, let alone God.

God has the plan. Not a plan or many plans to choose from if one doesn't work out. He has the plan. Before we were created, He planned exactly for us the whats, whens, and with whoms. You are part of the divine master plan. Thinking otherwise doesn't change the fact. In His plan is your purpose. Your assignment on earth.

You are specific for a specific purpose. Gifted you are. Talented? yes! Often, we spend time either criticizing or admiring talented people oblivious that within us are talents too. Believe it or not you are gifted. It matters not if another is more talented than you, there is a need for you and a space needed to be filled by only you to make maximum impact!

In simple terms you aren't "matter" having weight and occupying space here. For we are God's workmanship; created in Christ Jesus to do good works, which God prepared in advance for us to do.[1] God saw a need in this world and created you to meet that need. You need to find that purpose.

So how do you know your purpose?

Get online and take a strength and weakness test? Rate yourself to find the kind or the combination of personalities you are? Find out what you are passionate about? Find out what you do easily? Find what you are good at? Find what people will pay you for? What you would do if you have no obstacles? And there, you will know something about yourself and consequently your purpose? Maybe, maybe not.

The above strategic questions have been used and recommended by motivational speakers, counsellors and pastors. When you truthfully answer them, you are sure to notice some of your strengths and weaknesses but they do not point out your God-given purpose on earth. They simply don't! They may suggest you pursue engineering or medicine. They may suggest you become a pilot or an author.

Yet all engineers don't have the same weaknesses and strengths. All authors aren't choleric. All doctors aren't good at dancing. All evangelists aren't dynamic. No man-made test can be designed in a way to tell us exactly our purpose on earth.

Make a list of all your weaknesses, strengths, talents, skills and passion. Don't they suggest more than one purpose? If one clearly stands out, which often times is what we choose because we want it, which level do you even take it? Do you as a gifted singer produce albums for millions to enjoy across the entire world or be a worship leader in your church? Do you become an itinerant preacher or take care of a flock in a sheepfold church? Do you set up an orphanage home or home for the aged? Do you set up a company or not?

How do you even tell if it aligns with God's purpose for you? How do you know what your assignment here is? The curiosity of what to do and what not to do can be frustrating.

Truly, the purpose of a gift is sometimes unknown to the receiver. The receiver may use the gift for a purpose completely different from what the giver intended. Whereas the purpose of some gifts may be obvious to the receiver, he decides to use it for the obvious reason or not. For the purpose of the gift to be served and its benefits fully enjoyed, the receiver needs to know the intention of the giver.

I know without a shroud of doubt, the specific assignments for which we are given gifts, talents and abilities are known to God. After all, He created us.

So get on your knees in prayer and ask God. The truth is God puts passions in our hearts to stir us in a direction He desires. God gives us talents to use them in a way He desires. So only God can tell you exactly what He wants you to do with what He has given to you. He gives life for a reason.

Yet we will do anything than ask God. We want man-made principles. We want a set of questions which when we answer point us in a direction only God can. So we roam in circles. Try out jobs. Follow our hearts. We try to provide man-made solutions. We provide man-made water to quench divine thirst.

Here we are. Rich but unsatisfied. Smiling but hurting. Drowning but waving. Limping but dancing. Ahead but lost. Many people have died without knowing their exact purpose. Many have excelled in the wrong purpose too.

Ask Him today. God speaks in different ways. It can be through dreams, people, sermons, songs or in a clear audible voice. I have learnt one thing personally about God. He always confirms His word. Almost every word I have heard from God through a channel has been confirmed either through the same channel or another. He is faithful and doesn't want us to miss His path. So the word keeps coming in all directions until we recognise and obey.

Determined to please God? To be used by Him to

affect generations? To bring Him glory? Then ask Him what to do with these gifts and talents you possess. Nothing else matters when you know your God-purpose. No words can explain the feeling of knowing you are pleasing God.

I don't know whether fasting will get you the answer. I don't know whether all-night prayers will get you answers. This I know, that the heart that earnestly seeks God's direction will surely find it. Seek and you will find.[2] Have the patience to wait for His direction. He will definitely show you. I know so.

I hope you spend a week or so praying to know your purpose before you flip the next page. It doesn't matter if you have started on the wrong path. You can still turn around. It is not too late. It is better to get on the right path than go further on the wrong one. Oh, what joy when you find out you are on the right path. God is standing by with the right path.

There are many plans in person's heart but it is the Lord's purpose that prevails. Just ask Him.[3] Be Inspired!

3 SETTLE FOR GOD'S

Have you heard something from God? I mean concerning your purpose? It is important you take time to know. If you have or already know, write it here before you continue.

....
....
....
....
....
....
....
....
....

Whispers. Nods. Thumbs up. High-fives. These were seen among the people today. Affirmations here. Affirmations there. Even critics and sympathisers agreed. This man is special. The Prophet they have awaited.

Give Him anything ordinary and He adds extra to it to make it, well you know. Give Him nothing and He will use words. Yeah, simple words you and I use every day. He creates and heals with words. It wasn't a rumour. It actually happened. He used words chemically to change water into wine. The couple could have started a wine business with it. The wine was special. Ask the master of the banquet.[1]

Today, He used a boy's lunch to feed five thousand men. Kids and women weren't numbered. If I'm doing the statistics, let's just agree on ten thousand in all. There were left overs. Twelve baskets full.[2] Jesus is special. He could even defeat the whole Roman army with words. No argument.

So they all affirmed. The plan was simple. "Let's make Jesus, King." Ask Him and He will talk His way out. They knew. So they decided not to tell Him. They won't ask for His opinion. After eating the miraculous bread and fish, only God knows the strength they possessed now. Carrying Jesus will be a simple task. They were getting ready.

Before the crown specifications reached the goldsmith. Before the type of robe was decided on. Before they selected the men to do the swooping. Jesus was gone! Away into the mountains. Poor people. Before they thought, Jesus knew. He didn't stay to argue. He didn't stay to fight. He left.[3]

Every God-idea is a good idea but not every good idea is a God-idea. To be a King isn't a bad idea. It's a great idea but not God's purpose for Jesus. He was to be crucified for our atonement. Without the shedding of blood, there is no remission of sin.[4] The plan was put in place the genesis morning when sin entered the garden. Today, a tummy-full-health-restored people wanted to make Him King. They wanted to alter His divine purpose, so Jesus run. He left.

Here is the irony. Jesus is already Lord overall but they wanted to reduce him to rule one empire. Give people the chance and they will make you king over a colony when you are to rule the world.

When you find God's purpose for you, settle for it. Do everything you can to stay in it. There will be temptations to do otherwise. Well-meaning friends and family will cajole you into something else but don't barge. If it is God's, you have got nothing to worry about.

The purpose of God can sometimes be what's already burning in your heart. That's easy to follow. However, most times it can be frightening. So frightening it consequentially magnifies your inadequacy. It makes you want to bargain with God. You list excuses for the purpose to be given to another.

Moses admitted his inadequacy. A wanted man in Egypt. I doubt the bounty on his head had expired yet. Now God wanted him to be the cavalry to liberate the Israelites. You should understand his sluggishness. The two wonders God showed him didn't extinguish his fear. So Moses listed his flaws. Slow of speech. Slow of tongue. Ineloquent. There, enough reason to find someone else? Not for God. God brought Aaron to speak and told Moses, "...and I will be with your mouth and with his (Aaron) mouth, and I will teach you what you shall do." [5]

Then came Jeremiah. His age was the perfect excuse. He felt he was too young to speak. Even after God mentioned He knew him before he was formed in his mother's womb. And appointed him as a prophet unto the nation. God touched his mouth and put His words on his mouth to speak. [6]

Don't give excuses. Don't pursue your own agenda. Don't follow people. A venture which has made others successful won't make you successful. A wrong choice can lead to poverty, frustration, irresponsibility, loss of faith among many consequences. Settle for God's. He made you. Your catwalk is futile when you've got horse power. It will be nice but unproductive. Only God knows where you will be profitable. He will make use of you to the maximum.

Don't have to look far. There are gifted and talented people struggling in a certain choice of profession and ministry. Why? It is not God's purpose for them. Today, we have pastors messing up because someone thought their abilities to sing or lead opening prayer with such depth qualified them for the post. Someone thought their knowledge of scripture was a green light for ministry. Even hunger has inspired others. Now, not a single day passes without news of a Pastor messing up. It is sad.

Settle for God's. Will it be easy? No. Will you struggle? Yes. Will you fail? Many times. But once you are engaged in God's divine assignment, you can do all things through Christ who gives you strength.[7] His divine power has given us all things that pertain to life and godliness, through the knowledge of Him who called us by glory and virtue.[8] So don't give up. Don't stop. Don't you dare when it gets tough!

Settle for God's because one day you will give an account of how you used your gifts and talents. One day, books will be opened and every deed under the sun will be known. Heads will kiss crowns. Feet will tread on gold. That same day, teeth will gnash and eyes will weep forever in hell. You have what it takes to decide what happens to you that day.

There is only one way to get to heaven; Jesus! He is the way, the truth and the life and none shall come to the father except through Him.[9] He is the answer and you have to accept Him as your Lord and Personal Savior to gain access to heaven. It is either *heaven* or *hell*. I implore you to make the choice today if you haven't. Confess your sins and accept Him.

When you do God's bidding. When you lean on Him. When you obey and keep His word. You are assured of making impact. You end up affecting generations. You challenge people to turn to Christ, live right and consequently leave a meaningful lasting impression. Impression that puts you in the limelight among the saints in heaven. You prosper. Divine prosperity that transcends anything perishable.

Here, God's assurance through Isaiah.

"So do not fear, for I am with you; do not be dismayed, for I am

your God. I will strengthen you and help you; I will uphold you with my righteous hand. For I am the Lord, your God who takes hold of your right hand and says to you, Do not fear; I will help you."
Isaiah 41:10;13

God has promised to deliver you when you fall into trouble.[10] When the going gets tough, He's promised to be there. For our light affliction which is but for a moment works for us a far more exceeding and eternal weight of glory.[11] Like Moses and Jeremiah, your weakness only demands your dependency on God. God will take care of your shortcomings. Like Jesus, settle for God's. Run if need arises. Don't do anything else. Be Inspired!

4 COMPETITION

Plato has been credited with the quote, "Necessity is the mother of invention." In this 21st century, I think competition has become the mother of invention. Softwares are updated by the week. New phones with more features by the month. New models of cars by the year. Technology is barely static. Monopoly is no longer a word that describes a company's grip of the market for even a year. Too soon a competitor overtakes with an upgrade. Then another takes over. Ways to outsmart, grab a large market share and make huge profit are evident in this century.

Competition is inevitable on earth. It is everywhere. Where I live, there is a street that houses a chain of four stores each selling groceries. They open and close around the same time. Do they make profit? Well, because they all have been in business for the last three or so years, I guess yes. Competition is a good thing once it leads to providing better services.

So unless you live on an island alone, there are going to be people far advanced than you and vice versa serving the same purpose. That fact doesn't mean you should envy, scheme and destroy the other person. That fact cannot be the reason to remain idle because you are the least gifted one.

There is a purpose you have to fulfil which will lead to another's success. It will lead to a dream come true. It will take someone to their destination. The success of those ahead have cleared dusty paths and given legs to your dreams. When you fail to meet your purpose, you deny others the opportunity you had.

God in His infinite wisdom gave many same gifts and talents but to serve with our uniqueness. I have heard more than ten pastors preach on faith. I am awed at the depth, dimension and twist each presented the message. I have read and listened to innumerable strategies on leadership, entrepreneurship and writing. Each carried certain uniqueness owing to the author and speaker. I have heard different artistes sing the same song but with a unique graceful touch from each.

Yet we see hatred and envy among people with the same gifts, talents and abilities. We want right to exclusivity. It should be about us. We deserve the spot. It didn't start now.

This attitude started a long time ago. It began when the Israelites left Egypt. A young man came running to Moses. His message was simple. Eldad and Medad were prophesying in the camp. Joshua's face turned red. He asked Moses to stop them. Moses looked at Joshua. Joshua saw the expression on his face but Moses had to say it anyway, "Are you jealous for my sake? I wish that all of the LORD's people were prophets and that the Lord would put his Spirit on them."[1]

Joshua felt sorry. Which leader of the Israelites at that time wouldn't want all of them to prophesy? The least uncomfortable situation, they murmur and groan. Moses was frustrated. He wanted help but Joshua wanted exclusivity. The right to prophesy should be reserved for a few. Joshua was wrong.

Several centuries later, same thing happened with the disciples of Jesus. Proud to make *#TeamJESUS*. They were determined to maintain the right to preaching. You ought to be one of them to preach about Jesus. You better be a disciple to heal in His name. That right was reserved and protected by copyright.

They were wrong regardless of their passion and sincerity. They were blinded despite their love and dedication.

"Master," said John, "We saw a man driving out demons in your name and we tried to stop him, because he is not one of us," "Do not stop him," Jesus said, "for whoever is not against you is for you."[2]

Read the reply of Jesus again. Jesus didn't question their intention. He knew it already. He gave them a reason not to impede the man. Once this man is succeeding, he will carry on with his deliverance ministry. There is a possibility the disciples will meet him again. When they do, they should rather support him. They should support anyone at all with that same agenda. The harvest is plentiful but the workers are few.[3]

So yes! We are not here to compete with each other. We are not here to fight for a huge market share. We are not here to be the first to grab God's attention. We are here to serve with our uniqueness.

Even the most purchased book in the world hasn't seen some shelves in the author's country. No one author awes all readers. No speaker grabs all attention. No matter how great you are, you can't appeal to or be accepted by all. No matter how small you are, you can touch and transform someone. Work with your uniqueness. Work in the area of your strength as led by God.

The Reply of Jesus is the way forward for you and me with the same talents or in the same profession. Let's fix our eyes on the bigger picture. Let's help others be better. Let's train others without fearing they will overtake us. Yeah they may become better than us. Shouldn't we be happy about that? The goal is to touch and transform people. Let's not envy. Rather support and encourage for we face a common enemy. Be Inspired!

5 LET'S CELEBRATE OUR DIFFERENCES

You are a specific part of the whole. You are here to play a role. You have a spot in God's drama production. The drama which ends in mankind fully united with God in heaven. All the singular assignments are wired in a divine plan to achieve the ultimate goal.

The author, banker, conference speaker, teacher, engineer, baker and you have a link together. This link brings solutions to problems. It is meant to draw people to the saving grace of Jesus Christ. It is meant to inspire them to fulfil their assignments. Then one day, we all with one accord shall lift praise to God. Hallelujah!

On many occasions we have seen scientists, artistes and the best in all walks of life put together in a team to solve a problem facing a nation, debate a policy or appoint a leader. You don't think God put us here to solve a bigger problem? One greater than what plagues even a continent? He did.

God requires us to serve with our uniqueness and abilities harmoniously to achieve the goal. This should be simple.

Except we have allowed two problems to stand in the way.

First problem. We are concentrating on the other person instead of doing our work. Not even the same work. If it were the same purpose with same set of skills and talents, envy seems apparent. It is an inherent instinct. It is expected. We have dealt with competition in the previous chapter. However to envy someone whose purpose is totally different? Someone whose abilities and talents are different? It makes no sense.

I am an author. I have a banker as a brother. A teacher as a sister. A hair stylist as a cousin. Why should there be a spark of jealousy among us? Okay, I know what you are thinking. Our incomes aren't same. So are our needs and inward satisfaction which only God can tell.

She is a member of the choir. He is a prayer warrior. Another ushers. Why should there be room for envy? It makes no sense to me.

It is unfortunate when envy and jealousy take root amongst us. When we scheme to destroy an individual or a group engaged in something different. When we criticise not to correct but frustrate. When we throw insensitive slurs. When we lose sight of the common goal. When we focus on being petty. We end up giving less than our best in our work. We mess everything up.

Are we not one in Christ? Should our differences punch holes in our unity?

"There are different kinds of gifts, but the same Spirit distributes them. There are different kinds of service, but the same Lord. There are different kinds of working, but in all of them and in everyone it is the same God at work. All these are the work of one and the same Spirit, and he distributes them to each one, just as he determines." –
1 Corinthians 2: 4-5,11

Apostle Paul gives insight into the many gifts of the Holy Spirit. Different gifts given by the same God. The purpose is to edify the church. To show the power of Jesus. To depopulate the devil's kingdom. The diversity of the gift makes it easier to address every issue in the body of Christ.

Same can be said of our talents and skills. Imagine a country of only bankers. Where would they get the money to run it? Imagine only teachers. Who are they going to teach? Imagine only lawyers? Let's leave it. The diversity of our gifts and talents forms the bedrock of sanity in mankind.

Imagine a church full of only song ministers? Only ushers? Only instrumentalists? I am sure you get the picture. We should rather be challenged to stretch beyond ourselves than envy. We ought to celebrate our differences for harmonious living.

Second problem. We will play our role but only in the position as the head. We want to get to the top by all means necessary. We won't take orders from anyone. We see our current role as a demotion. We think we know what's right. We think we are better. We have become a separated entity in whole.

We may be right. We may be the creative one in the group. We may be the expert. We may be the strongest link except whiles we are busy pointing out flaws and demanding promotion; the overall work suffers. The objective isn't met. Resources are wasted since progress is replaced with sabotage. Humility with pride. Respect with hatred.

The truth is no matter our statuses and abilities in life, our purpose on earth will always be in front, behind or besides someone at every point in time. Paul reiterates the essence of minor or less honourable roles using the human body parts in this text.

"On the contrary, those parts of the body that seem to be weaker are indispensable, and the parts that we think are less honorable we treat with special honor. And the parts that are unpresentable are treated with special modesty, while our presentable parts need no special treatment. But God has put the body together, giving greater honor to the parts that lacked it, so that there should be no division

in the body, but that its parts should have equal concern for each other. If one part suffers, every part suffers with it; if one part is honored, every part rejoices with it." **1 Corinthians 2: 22-25**

"And whoever wants to be first must be your slave just as the Son of Man did not come to be served, but to serve and to give His life as ransom for many"[1] were the words of Jesus. He didn't mouth these words but demonstrated by washing the feet of His disciples. Our ability to lead depends largely on our ability to serve.[2]

So find your spot and give the best in you. Be the best neck if you are called to be neck. Be the best hand, if you are called to be hand. Don't be a miserable or weak head when you are called to be a great foot. No two people can be head at the same time.

When you become head, be influential. Be humble. Be common like Jesus. My big brother, Eric Atta-Sono wrote this on Facebook wall one day, "My dear friend, has it ever crossed your mind that Jesus, the Christ was equal to his disciples in every way, that even to be able to identify him for arrest, he had to be betrayed with a kiss? My dear friend, please think about this and purpose to be humble in the true sense of the word as we strive to follow his example as our Master."[3]

Let's learn to celebrate our differences. Let's challenge ourselves to give our best in whatever roles we are given. Let's be humble. Be Inspired!

6 THE HIGHEST YOU

We aren't here to compete. Neither are we to remain same. There is a highest you to attain. In fact there is the limitless, you till you die. There is more to what you see in your mirror today hidden and untapped.

Here is one problem. We easily get comfortable with our talents and abilities without sharpening it for greater impact. The applause gets to our heads. The praise makes us float. Yet the water on which we float is a pond a baby could walk through.

Next problem. We will take a step but too slow. It takes forever to act on an idea. We want all assurances before we move. But the long planning and calculation drains the passion. We fear losing. The cost is unaffordable. Someone whispers it can't be done. We buy in. We get bored. We abandoned the idea. We move on to the next. The circle continues. How many projects have we left undone?

Then there is, "Someway-Somehow" syndrome. A thinking pattern which makes people idle and ignorantly hope that everything will fall in place. Someway-somehow, the business will flourish. Someway-somehow, she will come back. Someway-somehow, I will get noticed. Someway somehow, the money will fall in the account.

Someway-somehow, I will get a job. Someway-somehow, I will lose ten pounds. Someway-somehow, I will pass this exam.

Here is the truth. Dirty shirts don't wash themselves. Keys don't turn themselves. Shoes don't polish themselves. Same way, dreams don't achieve themselves. Exams don't write themselves. Calories don't burn themselves. Ideas don't act on themselves. I hope I just woke you up.

Even with no anointing backing secular music artistes for example, they are able to dazzle millions with their songs, get paid for it and become famous in the process. They have become influential and a single message from them can even alter a whole national election. They take the pain to rehearse at odd hours. They even abstain from certain foods. They push themselves beyond normal. They invest in knowledge. They are disciplined.

Why must we settle for mediocrity? Why must we play small? Why walk with an in-built aircraft engine? When we even have the backing of the Holy Spirit? Why? And yes why should some dead fellow still reign as the greatest in something? And for so many years? When we have what it takes to be the greatest for and with God?

There is no excuse to remain idle. It is a must to get to the highest point in all we do.

How? Let me tell you. Shun comfort. Kill any, "Someway-Somehow" syndrome in your life. You need to stop working at your convenience only. Work with a sense of urgency. You need to step out and get out of bed. You need to stretch yourself beyond you. You need to risk making mistakes. You need to feel the pain.

You need to be disciplined to put your craft into work. You need to have the character and diligence to pursue your purpose. Do you see a man skilled in his work? He will stand in the presence of kings; he will not stand in the presence of unknown men.[1]

You need to invest in knowledge in your area of

expertise. You need basic knowledge in administration, accounting and investment. You need to learn. School yourself if possible. Information is now a click away. There are many free tailored online courses. Enrol and get knowledge to get to the highest you.

You need mentors. There are always pace setters in every field of endeavor. You may not afford their presence but perhaps their books, tapes and works. Get knowledge and learn from their experiences because by wisdom a house is built, and through understanding it is established; through knowledge its room is filled with rare and beautiful treasures.[2] Seek help but don't be like them. Don't walk in their shadows. Aim high and above. For no other reason than to make them proud. And the highest reason of putting a smile on God's face.

You need to surround yourself with accountable friends. Friends who will speak the truth without fear or favor. Friends who can shut you up when need be. Friends who can make you cease a course of action. Friends you will have a hard time convincing about some pleasurable choices you want to make. Friends who can remove the roof and lower you before Jesus when you are crippled by a situation.[3]

Seek more hands to help. No purpose on earth is achieved in isolation. Jesus had disciples. God already has people placed at vantage points to help. It is part of the plan. Like Jesus, ask God for direction to your helpers. Open up to seek hands to help. You will go far if you leave what you can't handle to people who can. Delegate and give people responsibility and power to work. More importantly, be grateful. Make sure you thank everyone for any support they give.

Have a teachable spirit. Ravi Zacharias mentioned, "Somehow you can get so sterile in your own thinking and in an autocratic form think you are prone to be living a life completely devoid of error. Don't despise the man or woman who comes to you and is daring enough to challenge you and tell you when they see your life going off course."[4] Needless to add to this be humble to accept your shortcomings. Work on your character flaws. Apologize when wrong.

Now finish whatever you have abandoned. Find the reason that fuelled your first step. Encourage yourself in the Lord. And pick up where you left off. Finish that script. Finish course. Finish that project. Let nothing stand in your way. You are built for a certain speed. Built for a certain standard. It should reflect in the way you carry yourself. Pay no attention to people determined to see you average. Keep company of inspirers and pushers.

Give your best to whatever you do. Ensure no one fails or suffers in your area of expertise as long as it depends on you. Be great in your calling. Joseph didn't fail Pharaoh in interpreting the dream. Daniel didn't fail King Belshazzar in interpreting the writings on the wall. David didn't fail in playing the harp to drive way King Saul's demons. These Kings were told about these gifted men of God who were known for excellence in their calling. The men delivered. Give your best.

Then pray. No one can underestimate the potency of prayer. Pray not only for opened doors but direction to those doors. Pray for strength. Pray for wisdom. Pray for anointing. Pray for the hand of God in your life. Give yourself to prayer.[5] Pray!

You can't be anyone. This leaves with you one option. Get to your highest point. Get to the peak of you. It might be the highest peak in the world, your country, community, church or even family. What matters is you get there. Not to compete with anyone but to reflect the glory of God. Be Inspired!

7 WHY WE ARE HERE

Do what you want! Prioritize your interests! Follow your passion! We hear these at seminars and in sermons. We read in books and magazines. We see on the TV screens and billboards. We see on social media. We see in the neighbor.

So we helplessly yearn for it. Except we make it about ourselves. What we want in a job. What we want in a spouse. What we want in life. Our way! After all, there isn't much to life. Here one day, out the next. Sincerely, how have we fared with such reasoning?

Truth be told, there are people who are doing good living as they want. They even serve hope every morning to people across the entire universe from a beautiful developed city to a hopeless remote village.

However, many wars which have plunged nations into severe hunger, incurable diseases and shattered dreams were as a result of one man's way.

A husband followed his heart and absconded with a mistress leaving the jobless wife to commit suicide. Now, a bleak and hopeless future awaits the kids.

Don't look far. A wrecked community! A collapsed business! A ruined church! A broken home! Someone wanted to have their way. Listen to the story behind the drug addict, rapist, homeless and armed robber. Chances are you would find someone's selfishness contributed to who they are now.

So why are we really here? To do what we like whether good or evil?

The answer provides a fundamental compass as to how to live each single day. You would find the answer in what the moon does with the sun's light. We are here to do same with God's glory. We, like the heavens exist to declare God's glory.[1]

Our talents, abilities and skills given for our assignment on earth are to bring God glory. God gave Joseph the ability to dream and interpret it before the butler, baker and Pharaoh dreamt. And Joseph told Pharaoh, God will be the one to give him an answer of peace not him. Joseph brought God glory.[2]

It hasn't been about us. It has always been about God. There is only one God, the Father, who created everything and we live for him.[3] I admit I have made it about me. Who hasn't? We do it without realising. Even our good acts satisfy a certain selfish ambition to be known, respected and exalted. It does feel good. Really it does!

Wouldn't God want us to be happy? Satisfied? Fulfilled? He does but He ask that we boast in him[4] because both riches and honor come from him.[5] He exalts one man and humbles the other.[6]

Therefore, whether you eat or drink or whatever you dodo all to the glory of God.[7] It is with this basic understanding we ought to live everyday as we fulfil our purpose on earth.

Let the entrepreneurs strategize with this basic understanding. Let the Pastor or church officer, lead with this thought in mind. Let the author, blogger, musician, doctor, engineer, banker, innovator, etc. go about their duties with this in mind. Let us relate to our spouses, colleagues, subordinates, business partners, friends and strangers with this in mind. Let's change the way we live with this thought and we can transform our generation.

I love reading autobiographies and biographies of great and wealthy men. The challenges they faced and how they overcame them. I have scribbled down some of their principles and practice them every now and then.

Are they glorifying God? Let's say yes. Investments that cover four generations. Job security. Charity work. Travels. Prestige clubs. Hall of fame. You add the rest. And I know if we could afford a thousand sunsets to swap roles, we would without thinking.

We likely wouldn't want to swap roles with the missionary whose body is deteriorating from diseases because of his work. Or the mother whose commitment is to nurture and train her daughters to make sure they find Christ at the expense of her own dreams. But is the missionary glorifying God? How about the mother? Let's say yes.

Now let's talk truth. Poor doesn't glorify God. Rich doesn't glorify God. The only thing which glorifies God is a life pointing to Him instead of you. It is fulfilling your purpose on earth. It lies in speeches and actions and inactions that acknowledge the hand of God behind the heights you attained.

Until you do what brings God glory, there will still be an unsatisfied thirst that will leave you awake at night though you smile at day. It will leave you silent though you parrot your views in the midst of people. No man-made water can quench a divine thirst.

So strategize to shape a future, build a legacy, touch humanity or simply bring a few smiles to a face but make sure the fundamental reason is to glorify God and not you. Then you have done right.

Now you know you are specific. You have a specific assignment. You are not in competition. You have to get to the highest you. You are here to glorify God. I am glad you read this book. A few lines to go.

Don't stop there. Reach out to people who are lost.

Spread the gospel. Time is running out. You don't have to go far to find someone struggling with their worth. A neighbor. A colleague. A supervisor. Help them find their feet in Christ. Tell them how specific they are in God. Let's get out.

Here is my prayer. I ask – ask the God of our Master, Jesus Christ, the God of glory - to make you intelligent and discerning in knowing him personally, your eyes focused and clear, so that you can see exactly what it is he is calling you to do.[8]

The Lord keep you. Don't lose your value in Christ. You are specific. Be Inspired!

POEM 1

My very own
The depths of human being are unfathomable
Linked to the Creator
He who is intrinsic, detailed
Impossible to replicate
Is the form of the human being

The mind the spirit
The undeniable personal touch that can never
be recreated
These are the intimate, ultimate gifts
Personally given
The package wrapped
Just for you
Your very own thoughts
Character…smile
You are yours alone

Made by the Almighty
Imaged from His own being
Breathing His own breath
You are your own beauty

YOUR ARE SPECIFIC

May then our spirit rise
To glory
To live
To conquer
To leave our own imprint on this earth
As it should be
As it must be

Naserian Jeanne
Copyright @ 2015

POEM 2

Creation had its chapters
Birds had songs
Insects had whispers
Trees had heights
Each creature had a dwelling
It was specific

Love keeps no records of sin
Love forgives and forgets
Love builds a future
Love gives hope
Love made you
Love made us
It is specific

Dreams become realities
Hope gives a better tomorrow
Perseverance achieve greatness
God's word is there to prove
His grace is sufficient to push
He's made it specific

Now I know

YOUR ARE SPECIFIC

When I can't simply understand
Why I am this way or that way
When I want to give up
When I want to join the crowd
I shouldn't
I dare not
Because I am specific

Abigail Acheampong
Copyright @ 2015

REFERENCES

Introduction
1.   John 17:4 NLT

Chapter One – Do You Remember?
1.   Gen 1: 26-27
2.   http://izquotes.com/quote/8615 retrieved on 17th July 2015
3.   1 Samuel 16, 17:28 KJV
4.   Hebrews 4:16 NKJV
5.   John 16:7-8
6.   Romans 8: 26-27 NIV
7.   2 Corinthians 12:9 NKJV

Chapter Two – Specific For A Purpose
1.   Ephesians 2 : 10 NKJV
2.   Matthew 7:7
3.   Proverbs 19:21

Chapter Three – Settle For
1.   John 2
2.   John 6: 5-13
3.   John 6: 14-15
4.   Hebrews 9:22 KJV

5. Exodus 4: 10-15 NKJV
6. Jeremiah 1: 4-9 NKJV
7. Philippians 4:13 NLT
8. 2 Pet 1:3 NKJV
9. John 14:6
10. Psalm 50:15.
11. 2 Corinthians 4:17

Chapter Four – Competition
1. Numbers 11:26-29
2. Luke 9: 49-50
3. Luke 10:2

Chapter Five – Celebrating Our Differences
1. Matthew 20: 27-28
2. John 13:1-11
3. Status Update - facebook.com/EricAtta-Sono retrieved 12th August, 2015

Chapter Six – Highest You
1. Proverbs 22:29 HCSB
2. Proverbs 24:3-4
3. Mark 2: 2-12
4. Ravi Zacharias Sermon, "Lessons from Royalty."
5. Psalm 119:4b KJV

Chapter Seven – Why You Are Here
1. Psalm 19:1 KJV
2. Gen 41:16
3. Corinthians 8:6
4. 2 Corinthians 10:17
5. 1 Chronicles 29:12
6. Psalms 75: 7
7. 1 Corinthians 10:31 NKJV
8. Ephesians 1:17-18 MSG

OTHER BOOK BY THE AUTHOR

"A laid down formality or thoughtful display of agape love? You decide!"

When we put all together, how far we've come, what we have survived, what we own; basically who we are now, only one thing makes sense IT HAD TO BE GOD!

Foreword by Apostle Dr. Michael K. Ntumy Fr. Chairman Church Of Pentecost, this book is a must have written in simple, readable, contemporary language to motivate you to thank God —everywhere, every time, every day and for everything, even when the odds seem to be against you.

Kindle edition is available on amazon.com

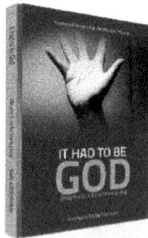

ABOUT THE AUTHOR

Kwabena Eddie Mankata - Is an author, playwright and speaker who believes we are here to do for God, what the moon does with sun's light - reflect His glory. He heads The Mankata Studios; Christian Company set to influence, challenge and empower its audience by providing pertinent biblical solutions to life issues through theatre, publications, talks and films.

His first book, "IT HAD TO BE GOD (Blueprint for a life of thanksgiving)" has received great recommendations and inspired many. He fellowships with Pentecost international Worship Centre, Sakumono where he is a Teen Teacher, President (Life Theatre), Executive Member (Prayer Ministry and Youth Ministry) and serves on a number of committees.

www.ingramcontent.com/pod-product-compliance
Lightning Source LLC
Chambersburg PA
CBHW071936020426
42331CB00010B/2902